AW

Amazon Web Services, the Ultimate Guide for Beginners to Advanced

Maverick Koston

TABLE OF CONTENTS

INTRODUCTION

A lot of the modern technology being introduced to the world today comes from the true visionaries of the past. Cloud computing is one of the modern-day concepts that can be traced back to the early 1960s and a scientist's idea of an "Intergalactic Network."

In a memo to some computer scientists, Dr. Licklider wrote about his version of an "intergalactic networking system." It was about a system that would support more than one user; it would possibly support thousands of computers. At the time Dr. Licklider wrote about his vision for the future, all the computers were still used for batch processing and computer time-sharing.

Back then he knew they did not, as yet, have the resources to accomplish his vision, but that never stopped him from pushing the future of computing towards it. Dr. Licklider's endless pursuit to build a computer networking system played an integral part in the creation of the Advanced Research Projects Agency Network

(ARPANET)

If you did not know it already, ARPANET was one of the first packet switching networks and was a division of the Department of Defence. ARPANET was also the first TCP/IP network and the base foundation of the internet as we know it today. The World Wide Web came to life on August 6, 1991, developed by Sir Tim Berners-Lee. Before he rewrote the code and released it as the World Wide Web, it was originally called the internet, and it was mainly used by scientists for easy access and sharing of data.

When Sir Berners-Lee's World Wide Web was created nearly three decades ago, it set a course that pushed technology into the realm of where it is today. It became a bridge between worlds, connecting people, corporations, and opening up a vast library of information about every subject imaginable. Today there is very little you cannot do or find over the web; in fact, nearly every modern-day household has access to it.

As technology grows and expands, so does the need for greater data capacity to handle the growth. The invention of the paperless office meant that more and more information needed to be stored on media. Not only was there a need for storage capacity to grow, but a need to share the information also grew too. On a business level, this meant the use of servers that could handle both the data capacity and data handling facilities. In larger corporations it meant large data centers and along with data centers came the need for backup facilities.

A network of physical computers and devices starts to get expensive, especially in a world that has to conform to various standards and compliances. As data is one of the company's most valuable assets, it needs to be secured and backed up in case of a disaster or mishap. Every few years all the equipment needs to be re-evaluated and upgraded, especially with how rapidly technology is evolving these days. The more evolved technology becomes, the higher the price of the equipment.

Mobile technology started to become an everyday part of both the business and public sectors. For business, it started to prove invaluable as more and more systems could be monitored or accessed from a tablet or phone. The shift towards mobile offices started to trend, and with this shift came the need for a more versatile way of staying connected to the office. In the public sector, it was a way of staying in touch with family, friends, and eventually to a host of followers.

Being able to connect with the world, stay in touch with the world, and gain access to applications online is the accepted norm in today's world. In fact, there is an app for pretty much anything today. With apps comes the need to store all the data you collect through that app. For instance, downloads of music, movies, photos, and so on all require quite a lot of space to store. You may have already noticed this, but lately, the more powerful computers are getting, the smaller their drives seem to be getting. There are external hard drives, SD cards, and flash disks, all media that can be used to store data on and give a person that extra storage space. But just like that hard drive in your computer, they are just as vulnerable to corruption, and maybe even more so. How many times can you remember dropping a hard drive or plugging one in to find it had given up on life?

There is some debate as to who coined the phrase "cloud computing," although in one networking diagram the internet was depicted by a drawing of a cloud, connected to the network with a lightning bolt.

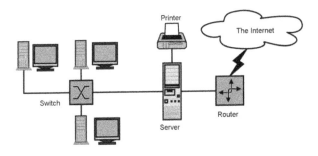

CompuServe was one of the first-ever ISP companies. It was founded in 1969 as a company that provided computer time-sharing. It was also known for its data processing services. In 1983 CompuServe customers enjoyed a small storage space on the CompuServe servers where they could store any types of files.

Although no longer in existence, CompuServe offered the first online ISP services experience and, if you will, a form of cloud computing. AT&T launched its business as well as personal communications platform, called PersonaLink Services, in 1994. PersonaLink Services was one of the first services to offer an all web-based storage solution. In their commercials, they referenced their web-based conferencing services as "our electronic meeting place in the cloud."

Today cloud computing is an industry that is pushing the bounds of billions of dollars a year for cloud hosting companies. As industry's demand increases, as well as personal usage demand for more storage space, the industry is expanding in leaps and bounds. For not only does a cloud computing environment offer space to purchase on the fly, but the data is also accessible anytime from any place, and if your PC crashes, you won't lose your data. With fast access to data from anywhere in the world and unlimited scalable storage, secure cloud computing is fast replacing conventional methods.

One such cloud service is Amazon Web Services (AWS), one of the world's leading cloud platforms and host to some of the top internet brands, like Netflix, Expedia, and Slack, to name but a few.

AWS: Amazon Web Services, The Ultimate Guide for Beginners to Advanced offers insight into cloud computing and what AWS has to offer.

CHAPTER 1
CLOUD COMPUTING

B efore local area networks (LAN) or wide area networks (WAN), companies outsourced their computer data processing to companies that had large mainframe networks. These services were mainly for items such as payroll runs and accounting services. Data was sent well in advance, as it took the data services companies weeks or so to prepare.

With the rise of personal computers and local area networks, then eventually wide area networks, companies kept all their data processing in-house. This would mean having a secure in-house local area network along with a wide area network if the business spanned regions or continents.

Local and wide area networks also mean major equipment outlays that either affected the company's capital expenses (CAPEX) or as an operating lease. Either way, equipment is expensive and it has to be maintained, as well as upgraded, on a regular basis. The data on the equipment needs specialized backup equipment. This is to ensure data continuity in order to minimize downtime in the event of equipment failure or disaster.

As companies strive for a leaner operating environment that offers more stability and flexibility while minimizing costs, they are moving towards cloud computing. Another way to look at it is that computing has looped back around to the good old days of computer outsourcing—only on a much larger scale with more control over the systems and data.

But it is not only organizations moving towards cloud computing; it is also widely used in the personal sector. People are finding cloud computing apps more convenient to use, less space-consuming, and better to back up their data. Apple has the iCloud, and Android users find using Google Drive or Dropbox easy for backing up their devices. The ever-popular Kindle uses Amazon Web Services to archive users' data.

The cloud is not only used for storing applications and data, it is also used to create programs, host websites, or run web services such as Airbnb, Netflix, or Lionsgate media services, and complete networking services for corporations.

What Is Cloud Computing?

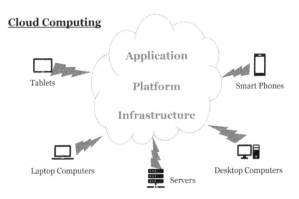

Cloud computing is a way to cut down costs, secure data, always have access to your applications, and offer data storage as or when you need it. It is a data storage, access, sharing, and application platform over the internet.

The Need for Cloud Computing

Historically, when you wanted an application, you would go and buy it off the shelf in a store. It would come in the form of a disk with some instruction manuals. You would put the disk into your computer and install the program onto it.

All the data, such as pictures, spreadsheets, documents, and various files would be stored on your computer's hard drive or some external media such as CDs, DVDs, external hard drives, SD cards, or flash drives.

But there is only so much space on those devices, which ultimately means having a library full of them, depending on how much data a person has. These days, rarely anyone carries their laptop around with them since it is so much more convenient to carry a mobile device.

The Need for Personal Cloud Usage

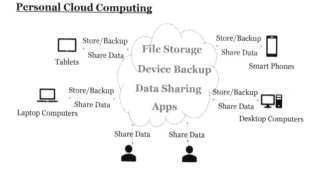

Modern-day personal devices only have so much storage space before you have to download your data to a disk. There is nothing more annoying than needing some information but having the wrong disk or forgetting it entirely.

With all the applications in use for mobile devices, a device can run out of storage space quickly. There are extra storage add-ons a person can use, such as an extra memory card. But, as with other storage devices, the sizes are limited and only one add-on per device can be used.

Mobile devices can be backed up onto computers or these extra storage devices, and if looked after, they can last. But your data is not too secure and any apps you may need instant access to will have to be reinstalled. If you need access to your data fast, it is not going to happen, as the data first has to be downloaded from the storage device.

The more reliant people have become on their devices, the more a need arose for quick access to their data and applications. As mobile devices tend to contain everything from schedules to documents or presentations, losing the device can be quite disastrous. The need became obvious for a more secure solution to backup, store, and quickly access applications.

A definite need for a storage facility where data could

be stored and accessed at any time, shared with others, or shared across devices was evident. Cloud computing was the solution since users get to choose the size of storage they need. They only pay for the storage they use, and they can share information across the internet and between devices. Users of cloud-based storage also have access to cloud-based applications.

The Business/Organizational Need for Cloud Computing

Business/Organizational Cloud Computing

For companies, the need for data storage grows exponentially each year. Thus when they are installing a networking system, they need to ensure that the system will cope for at least three years, or until their next upgrade date.

In a perfect world, an organization can usually scale its systems in order to budget for this growth. But things can change. Especially in today's economic climate, systems become outdated rather rapidly, as does software. If an organization does not keep up with these changes, they are leaving themselves open to security risks and the possibility of incurring greater costs to the business.

IT equipment becomes expensive for small, medium, and large-sized organizations. It is not only the networking infrastructure that has to be kept updated but their in-office equipment as well. In order for staff to be able to work efficiently and effectively, their systems need to be able to keep up with the networking equipment.

It can get even more expensive when there are staff members who constantly travel and need access to the servers. Traveling for staff members can become burdensome if they have to carry extra drives around with them or need to be near a corporate office to be able to access the company's network.

Hosted cloud platforms are the way a lot of companies

are moving because they could cut down the cost of a large data center. Disaster recovery is no longer a major issue, as the systems are located in the cloud, offering more resilience. Employees have easy, secure access to the system with nothing more than a registered PC and internet access.

Storage is bought on an as or when required basis that does not require expensive equipment purchases. The purchase and distribution of applications is more controlled, with a more streamlined updating procedure.

The Advantages of Cloud Computing

Cloud computing offers the following advantages for both business and personal use.

Scalable

Cloud computing offers scalable solutions that do not restrict the size, capacity, or performance of the system. If more storage is required, it is allocated on the fly and the cost added to current cloud computing capacity.

Cost-Effective

Cloud computing is cost-effective in that it can

considerably cut down on the costs of equipment and software. For start-up companies with limited resources or budgets, cloud computing could give the company an edge over its competitors.

It is a scalable system that allows for the purchase of space as and when needed. If you need more space, it will be added on at much less cost than it would take to upgrade a system. The good thing about pay as you go storage is that if it is found that the storage is no longer needed, it can be reduced, along with that cost.

There are a few different types of payment packages that vary for corporate or personal contracts. There is also a pay-per-use solution that helps with tight budgets or the need for temporary guests on the network.

Moving to cloud computing will also cut down the cost of having trained personnel to monitor, maintain, and run the systems. All the technical work is done on the side of the hosting company.

High-Speed Access and Deployment

Cloud computing provides high-speed access to your system, faster system deployment time, quicker systems downloads, and instant access to software/apps without having to do a full disk or download install.

24/7 Access From Anywhere at Anytime

The system is available 24/7, 365 days a year from anywhere in the world, as long as there is a reliable internet connection. This makes remote staffing solutions or home-based staffing solutions more simplified.

Reliability

As the host company would have fallback and switchover systems in place, they are able to offer a more reliable and stable system. Cloud hosting companies will offer various service level agreements (SLA) as part of their contract. These agreements determine the service level; some contracts have 1 hour, 2 hours, 24 hours, and so on for service level turnaround times.

Secure Backup

All the data and applications are kept in the cloud. They are regularly backed up by the hosting company in case the hosting company has a situation. As the data is not stored on-site local to the business or for personal use, it will remain unaffected by local systems downtimes and situations.

Resilient Disaster Recovery

Most disaster recovery procedures will have at least 12 to 48 hours of downtime before recovery unless there is a full fallback system located off-site. Off-site disaster recovery centers are very expensive, as they require a mirror setup of the company's current system.

Even systems that have these fallback centers or another off-site location may suffer data loss due to the timing of the disaster and method of data synchronization. On the other hand, when the whole system is accessed through the cloud, including shared data and applications, there is minimal chance of any data loss. The data and applications are available online from anywhere, even from a user's home, provided they have an internet connection. This makes data recovery a lot more resilient and systems downtime minimal.

Easy Cross-Functional and International Collaboration

Using the cloud platform allows for cross-team and remote office collaboration. It is easy and secure for team members from all over the world to work together from any location.

For personal use, this means easy access to data shared with family or friends, movies, music, and so on.

Virtualization

Virtualization in cloud computing allows for the sharing of different applications across different platforms for various companies or users.

Systems Independence

Having a cloud-based system means that an organization is not tied down to one particular location. Moving to another location is not as costly because there are minimal systems to be moved and there does not have to be a dedicated server or data center room.

Since any device that conforms to the minimal system's specifications can connect to the system, costly workstations with significantly large hard drives are no longer necessary. With the cloud acting as the network platform, as long the device is compatible with the software, data can be accessed even from an authorized smart device.

Advanced Security Features

As it is their business and the need to protect not only their system plus those of their clients, cloud hosting facilities have advanced security systems to ensure that data stays safe and secure.

The Types of Cloud Computing

There are four types of cloud deployment models and three types of cloud computing services. This section explains each cloud deployment method and the cloud computing service.

Deployment

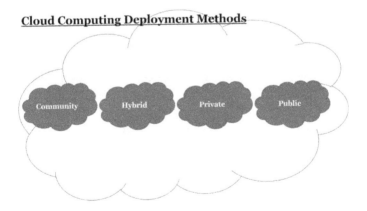

Cloud Computing Deployment Methods

Community   Hybrid   Private   Public

Choosing a deployment model is one of the first cloud computing decisions to be made. There are a few different deployment model types but the four main ones are the most widely used ones.

A deployment model is the cloud-based environment of the customer's choice. This environment includes various configuration, storage, proprietorship, costs, resources, and company needs.

Think of the deployment method as choosing a data center to outsource the companies IT networking solutions. Once a deployment method has been chosen, it makes the rest of the decisions that much easier to assess.

Community Cloud

Cloud Computing Community Deployment Method

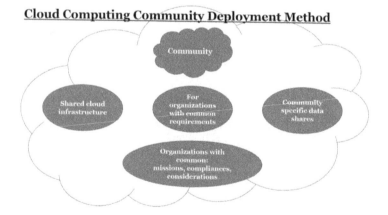

The community cloud offers similar features as that of the private cloud mixed with a few public cloud features. Yet the community cloud infrastructure is not shared with the public, but rather with several organizations that are

20

either a subsidiary of the other or have common goals and are known to each other.

Each organization is responsible for its own infrastructure and they will have shared resources such as software and common shared data or various mission statements, policies, etc.

The community cloud is ideal for organizations that have common interests or concerns such as religious organizations, medical organizations, various scientific research centers, farming communities, and so on.

Each organization may have its own private data access, shared applications, policies, legal requirements, and shared data. This cuts down on costs, administration, and duplication of work, ensuring that any common compliances, policies, etc. are adhered to and are correct.

Hybrid Cloud

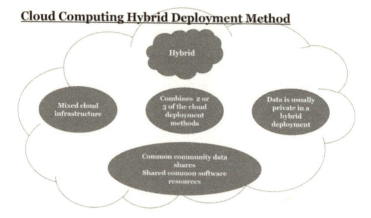

Cloud Computing Hybrid Deployment Method

Hybrid

Mixed cloud infrastructure

Combines 2 or 3 of the cloud deployment methods

Data is usually private in a hybrid deployment

Common community data shares
Shared common software resources

The hybrid cloud is made up of two or more of the deployment cloud methods. This method is the most flexible out of all the methods, as it offers an organization the ability to share public resources, share community resources with a selected group, and still keep their sensitive data or any proprietary software private.

Private Cloud

Cloud Computing Private Deployment Method

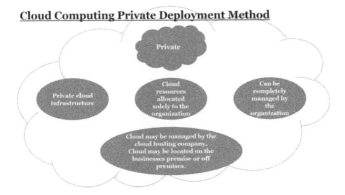

The private cloud is for the sole use of one organization. All resources, shared data, and sensitive data are accessible only by the organization that controls the private cloud. It is not the most cost-efficient solution, but it offers the greatest security, reliability, and stability out of all the deployment models.

Public Cloud

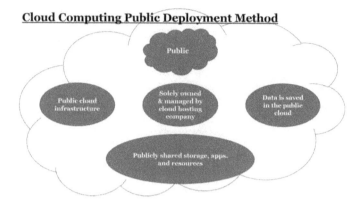

Cloud Computing Public Deployment Method

Public

Public cloud infrastructure

Solely owned & managed by cloud hosting company

Data is saved in the public cloud

Publicly shared storage, apps. and resources

This is the deployment method that is most widely used and is broadly considered as "the cloud." It is used by both individuals and businesses who are in need of shared resources. It is the most cost-effective of all the cloud deployment methods and requires the least security.

The services that are used can be pay-per-use, but the cloud is managed by the third-party company that owns the cloud.

Services

Cloud computing offers three different types of services, each offering a company or end users different components. The service required will depend on the consumer's needs whether they are business or end user.

Cloud Computing Services

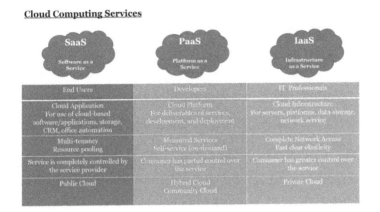

Software as a Service (SaaS)

This is the most popular service model for cloud computing, used by both end users and businesses. The service is managed completely by the cloud service provider. The cloud service provider hosts a number of applications which are made available to end users or business that are signed up for the SaaS model.

Saas is the public transport of the services. It is convenient, cost-effective, and you get where you want to go. But you are limited to their routes, time frame, and service providers. Public transport is used by thousands of others all taking the same public transport as you do.

Still, you get to choose which transportation you use, scaled to the costs that suit your pocket, and the routes you want to use.

The operating system, applications, storage, networking, data, virtualization, runtime, and middleware are all offered as a service. These services are managed with pooled resources, over which the end user or business has no control. Any customizations or additions are organized and done by the service provider.

SaaS is also the easiest out of all the service models to use and comes with pay-per-use options which makes it attractive for the personal sector or smaller businesses.

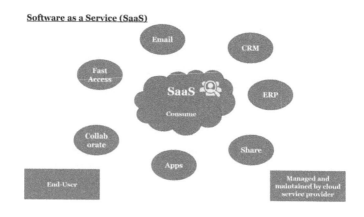

Software as a Service (SaaS)

Platform as a Service (PaaS)

Platform as a Service is mostly used by developers that design applications. It is also used for various companies that offer services.

Paas is like using a regular taxi service company. You have control over which car you would like to suit your transport needs. You have control over your destination, even your route. Although you don't share the taxi at the same time as others, it is still a shared resource.

The operating system, storage, networking, virtualization, runtime, and middleware are all offered as a service. These services are managed with pooled resources which the consumer/business has no control over. They are offered as a service by the service provider so any changes or additions will be controlled by the service provider.

Data and applications are managed by the consumer or business which means they have complete control over them. PaaS offers the consumer or business partial control over the hosted services.

Infrastructure as a Service (IaaS)

IaaS offers infrastructure as a service and is for companies or organizations that need a more secure environment for their data. Organizations that choose IaaS have complete autonomy over the software, operating system, storage, and so on. Some large scale organizations may even choose to host their own cloud-based solutions.

IaaS is more like a long-term lease or rental car. The business may not own the car outright but they have almost full control over it. An added benefit is that there are minimal to no maintenance costs on the car, as that is done by the lease or rental agency. Plus the car can go just about anywhere without restricted routes or having to conform to public or taxi transport rules. Your space is completely your own and not shared by the public or other businesses.

The operating system, storage, networking, servers, and virtualization are offered as managed services by the cloud hosting service. The runtime, middleware, data, and applications are managed by the consumer or business, which means they have complete control over them.

IaaS offers the consumer or business significantly more control over the hosted services than SaaS and Paas.

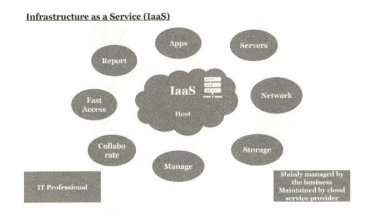

Infrastructure as a Service (IaaS)

CHAPTER 2
AMAZON WEB SERVICES (AWS)

A mazon Web Services is the leading secure cloud service provider, holding a 40% market share for its IaaS and PaaS services.

What Is AWS?

Amazon Web Services offers its clients scalable, affordable, and secure hosted cloud-based platforms. These services offer individuals or companies data storage, databases, web-based applications, and content delivery. A cloud-based networking platform offers companies a whole host of affordable solutions that could significantly cut operating costs while not limiting systems growth.

AWS offers different packages designed to suit the needs of both their business and personal clients. The storage, applications, and features depend on the cloud-based solution package a consumer chooses.

One of the most advantageous points of AWS is that it is scalable and it allows for pay-per-use options. If you need more storage, you can increase your package, and you can also decrease it, should you no longer need the storage capacity.

A Brief History of AWS

Amazon Web Services' first launch of EC2, Elastic Compute Cloud, was between 2003 and 2005, when they gave a select handful of customers access to the facilities while it was in its beta stage.

In 2006, Amazon released Amazon S3 (a storage service), Amazon Simple Queue Service (a data flow service), and Amazon SimpleDB (a database service) to the public. These services were rolled out and defined by zones/regions. In order to access or use one of these services, you first have to check what region and zone you fall under. Some services are not available in certain regions or zones.

In 2008, the beta phase of AWS services was replaced by service-level agreements in alignment with the launch of a few new cloud-based services. Some of the new features included are availability zones, local zones, and Elastic IPs to allow for better systems uptimes and redundancy. Along with these new features, CloudWatch, elastic load balancing, CloudFront, Elastic Block Store, Simple Notification, Route 53, and autoscaling were introduced to the public.

At the launch of these new services in 2008, AWS took on customers such as Zynga, Netflix, Reddit, and newcomers Airbnb, as well as Pinterest.

In 2011 through 2013, AWS had a few glitches, which caused major downtimes for companies relying on their cloud-based system. These were glitches that they could not afford with Microsoft Azure slowly making its mark on the cloud-computing industry. Close behind Azure, IBM cloud also started to gain popularity within the cloud-computing marketplace.

From 2014 through 2019, AWS has continued to add regions, improve upon its services, and hold its position as one of the top cloud-based service providers.

The Advantages of AWS

There are many advantages to moving to AWS. One of the most obvious is that they are the market leader in cloud-based services. They are also a corporate giant, an organization that spans the globe and has a presence in over 190 countries. They have long since gone through all their teething problems with cloud-based services and can confidently offer stability, reliability, and resilience.

Some of the main advantages of AWS are:

Reduction of Infrastructure Costs

With little to no IT infrastructure overheads in the form of expensive networking equipment, AWS gives smaller businesses the chance to leverage better equipment. That is equipment that they would not otherwise be able to afford due not only to the cost of the equipment but also the manpower to run it.

All equipment is the property of AWS and as such is monitored as well as maintained by them.

No Long-Term Commitment

There are no long-term contracts or even monthly ones. The services that are server backed services are charged on an hourly basis. While you are using them, they will be charged, but as soon as you stop using them, the charges stop.

No Equipment Procurement Delays

Ordering equipment can take months, not only to deliver it but to get approval for it, have it financed, and ordering it. Delivery of equipment, depending on any vendor agreements, can take anywhere from 3 to 12 weeks to arrive.

Cloud-based services cut out the procurement step, as all AWS needs is the requirements. The company needs to choose a deployment method, service, sign up, and everything is up in a lot less time than if an owned system were ordered.

Instant Access to Software

Software is also a lot easier to procure with AWS. There is no need to buy separate licenses. AWS has an extensive marketplace where you will most likely find cloud-based versions of the software required.

Scalable Infrastructure and Storage Solution

Pay-per-use allows for flexible scalable storage solutions. You pay only for what you use, and if you need more you can scale up. If you no longer need all that space, it is just as easy to scale down and stop paying for what you are not using.

With AWS, setting up a network infrastructure is not as hard to assess, scope, and get set up than with an actual on-premise network. AWS offers Amazon Machine Images service, which is an excellent way to expand the business infrastructure with cloned images that are ready in a fraction of the time a normal IT service environment would take.

Various Programming Language APIs

AWS has various programming language APIs, which makes them a very powerful commodity to have in the cloud environment.

Security and Stability

AWS has a sophisticated internet and physical security system. This offers the customer peace of mind and offers stability.

Reduction of Systems Maintenance Costs

For all AWS cloud-based systems, Amazon Web Services is responsible for the maintenance, upgrades, and monitoring of systems. This takes away the daily stress or cost of managing an IT infrastructure system.

Uses of AWS

AWS has become quite the driving force behind the internet infrastructure and can basically do anything online that a normal computer can do offline.

Here are few businesses uses for AWS:

Content Delivery Network (CDN)

A CDN is used to evenly distribute content to all parts of the world seamlessly. CloudFront is AWS' content delivery network service and offers this service at a better price than many other cloud hosting services do. CloudFront is highly flexible and has no scale limit to it.

Web Hosting

AWS may not be the cheapest web hosting option, but they offer a lot more flexibility and scalability than other hosting sites do. AWS offers great website launching tutorials to help get a website up and running.

AWS Email

AWS offers an easy-to-use and intuitive transactional email service called Simple Email Service (SES). This service can handle large-volume emails sent from the company email system.

Large Files

Sending large files through email or even over most web-based services is not only costly but also time-consuming. It gets rather frustrating waiting for the minutes tick by as the file gets sent, only to have it rejected because it was too large or the service timed out.

AWS has a service called S3, which stands for Simple Storage Service. This service is designed to handle, store, and share large files. It can also handle small files that need to be shared with a large group.

Well-Architected Framework

AWS designed the Well-Architected Framework to help its end users to understand the consequences of their decisions when building systems in an AWS environment. The Framework teaches the end user about AWS architecture and the best practices therein. AWS' Architect Framework tool aids with the designing of cost-efficient systems that are stable, reliable, efficient, cost-effective, and secure on AWS.

The framework tool brings a way for the end user to measure how their systems architecture measures up to the best practices as outlined by AWS. This pinpoints areas of weaknesses, vulnerabilities, and where there is room for improvement. AWS believes that business success depends on having a well-architected system.

AWS designed the architecture best practices from their years of collective experience in architecting solutions for a host of use cases as well as businesses. Since the inception of AWS in 2006, AWS architectural engineers have had thousands of their customers develop robust business solutions by using their architectural best practices model.

The AWS Well-Architected Framework works with a set of documented foundational questions in order to ascertain an organization's specific requirements and needs. These questions also reflect whether or not the architectural needs of the company align with the best practices of the AWS cloud architectures.

The framework describes the AWS strategies and best practices in their approach to operations and design of a cloud-based system. As such it is specifically designed for the use of IT chief technology officers, developers, and infrastructure architects.

AWS supplies a full set of documentation to help IT professionals with the AWS Well-Architected Framework tool. AWS reviews the workload for its customers at no extra cost and the service is easily accessible in the cloud to offer valuable information, statistics, and improvement recommendations.

Most IT professionals who have used this tool find that it helps to ensure that workloads are secure, efficient, more reliable, and cost-effective for the organization.

AWS also provides the Well-Architected Labs. This takes the form of a documentation library and a repository of code. This tool helps end users effectively and efficiently apply best practices. These documents help give IT professionals well-guided instructions, which also enables them to get hands-on experience with AWS.

Along with Well-Architected Labs, AWS has a set of general design principles from the Amazon Partner Network or APN Partners.

AWS General Design Principles

There is a set of general design principles that should be kept in mind which the AWS Well-Architected Framework can identify and that will ensure an optimal design in the AWS cloud.

Design Principles

Stop guessing capacity requirement: On-premise IT systems' capacity is designed by using estimations from past and present capacity statistics. The architecture of this IT system will then be based on an estimated growth rate. When the system has been procured and deployed, the organization runs the risk of either having underestimated the capacity or overestimating it.

Either way, it ends up being costly. An underestimation is going to incur non-budgeted costs, while overestimations mean the company sits with expensive equipment it is not making full use of.

In the AWS cloud environment, a company will not

have this problem, as capacity requirements are scalable on an as and when you need an extra capacity basis. This is called an elastic approach to capacity requirement. Just as easy as it is to expand the capacity, it is just as easy to decrease it. This ensures that the organization is only using the capacity it needs.

Production scale testing: With the ability to scale systems capacity and create virtualization instances, AWS makes testing products on a production scale doable. It is quick and easy to create a test environment to mimic a full production environment. This can be done on demand, and when the testing is done the instance and services will be decommissioned. This allows developers to test the products in a mirror of the production environment without incurring huge expenses and only paying for the usage of the test environment whilst it is still operational.

Architectural experimentation is easier when it is automated: With the rise of processes such as Lean and DevOps, one rule of thumb pops up a lot in the IT development world—automation. If a process, service, or function can be automated, it should be, as this cuts down on the impact and cost of human error. AWS allows for a low-cost way to automate the end user's system. The automation process has an easy but comprehensive reporting system that can audit the impact of changes to the system and can intelligently revert back to the previous versions or parameters if the need arises.

Be open to changes and allow natural evolution of architecture: Being able to test applications on demand lowers the risk of errors due to design changes. Automating these tests saves on both time and costs, as well as allows the system to naturally evolve over time.

Use data to drive architecture: Data in the cloud is measurable and as such allows the company to collect valuable data on the impact of the design architecture. This architecture is what affects workload behavior in the system. This data lets the end user make informed decisions that are fact-based on how to improve or balance the infrastructure workload.

The Five Pillars of AWS Well-Architected Framework

When you think of constructing a building, the first thing that needs to be done is the foundation.

Foundations, no matter what they are, should always be solid, well laid out, and made with the correct materials. You would also not build a house without a good set of plans.

The same approach is taken when designing a systems architecture. In AWS there are the five pillars of the architecting framework. These five pillars should always be taken into consideration to cut down on any challenges or problems that may arise otherwise.

By incorporating the five pillars into any IT architecting design framework, you will build a solid, secure, robust, and reliable system. When you build the system, it is always best to build with a structured approach.

Operational Excellence

Operational excellence is focused on how the system works and how the system is monitored. By continuous improvement and constant feedback in the form of user data, automated data logs, and various logged events, the system can use this information to address security risks, implement necessary changes, and strengthen system design weaknesses. The pillar stands for responding to events, automating changes, and managing changes and streamlining processes with the goal of operational excellence.

Security

Security focuses on the protection and integrity of the company's data and systems. Data needs to be kept confidential and secure by understanding the security risks. Establishing the correct security levels and monitoring system to suit companies' needs is the primary goal of the security pillar.

Reliability

The system should have a high uptime rate and a resilient, if not transparent, fallback procedure. This should set into action a plan that allows for minimal to no systems downtime in the event of a systems outage for whatever reasons. All efforts should go into preventing failures while also providing a built-in recovery procedure to get the system's backup running within a respectable amount of time.

Performance Efficiency

This pillar is focused on the performance of the system

as measured against the resources allocated to it. This pillar is a great way to measure if the system is operating to its optimal ability and providing the organization with the resources it needs to operate effectively.

Cost Optimization

Running an efficient system is not all about the system; it is also about the costs. By utilizing some of AWS' analytical tools, an end user can analyze and control operational costs. This is done by cost optimization in order to avoid unnecessary expenditure by keeping costs low. Understanding where the money is being spent and keeping tight control of the budget will help with not overspending on unnecessary services, applications, or solutions.

Why Corporations Are Moving to AWS

AWS offers little overhead while offering state-of-the-art server technology infrastructure in a cloud. Amazon is one of the oldest and therefore more experienced cloud-based hosting services. AWS also has a large coverage that spans the globe and hundreds of cities, and it is growing each year.

With a system that is scalable, cost-effective, and that can be in-house or hosted off-site, AWS is a very tempting prospect. This is especially true for smaller to medium-sized businesses or start-ups.

Global Corporations Using AWS

Right from the start, some big brand name companies such as Netflix used AWS services. Some of the larger well-known brand names and big organizations using AWS services are:

Netflix

Netflix has been loyal to AWS from the beginning. Netflix is an online streaming service that streams movies, TV series, reality shows, documentaries, and so on. It can be used on just about any internet-connected device that can handle video streaming.

UK Public Sector

AWS services public sector companies such as the DVLA, NHS, Barclays, and the UK Ministry of Justice.

NASA

NASA uses AWS for the Curiosity rover. Live streams

are streamed through AWS from the Curiosity Rover which has been on Mars since 2012.

Expedia

Expedia is the largest online travel company, with millions of online travel, holiday, and car rental bookings made through the site every year. It is also a long-running company that was launched in 1998. AWS is the platform it uses mainly for customers in the Asia Pacific region.

Adobe

Adobe uses AWS to help with the deployment of its enterprise applications such as Connect and LiveCycle.

Lionsgate Entertainment

One of the most successful film studios in North America is Lionsgate Entertainment. They have been making use of AWS services such as EC2 and S3 since 2010.

Airbnb

Airbnb is a relative newcomer to the Internet but is one of the most trending travel sites on the web these days. They have their entire database hosted on an Amazon Web Services database, called Relational Database

Service or RDS.

Yelp

Yelp is an online review and directory services company that allows customers to rate various services, especially restaurants. It was started in 2004 and makes use of Amazon Web Services to help with runtimes and increasing systems productivity.

Novartis

Novartis is an innovative medical company, based in Switzerland, that makes use of AWS tools in various screening tests.

Pfizer

Pfizer is a pharmaceutical company that produces over 160 medications and is known worldwide. They make use of AWS services such as EC2 and Amazon VPC.

Dow Jones & Company

Dow Jones & Company is one of the most well-known and biggest financial news companies throughout the globe. The company moved to AWS to make use of EC2 in their data center.

Nokia

Nokia, one of the oldest mobile phone companies, uses AWS in order to help with a scalable solution for their systems.

What Is Big Data and How Does AWS Use It?

"Big data" is a term used in the computer world to describe extremely large amounts of data that can be either structured and unstructured. This data may exceed a current system's processing capacity, by being too large or requiring too short a window for rendering.

An example of big data is records that are not complete or are not quite accessible due to the sheer volume of them. This could be census data of all the people in a certain country for generations. These records would more than likely come from various sources collected throughout the years.

The volume of data that is usually considered big data would be data spanning sizes of terabytes to petabytes. It has three basic common concepts called the "three Vs of big data."

The Three Vs of Big Data

Variety

Variety is data that is collected from different places such as social media, online shopping, forums, website subscriptions, surveys, and so on.

Velocity

This is how often big data is needed to be sorted, analyzed, processed, stored, and actioned. This could be anywhere from weekly updates, daily, and real-time statistics.

Volume

This is how large the data is, and this measure is counted in terabytes to petabytes of information.

AWS and Big Data

Most companies should have a strategy for handling big data, as it will help them to keep their costs down and have effective procedures that help to efficiently process as well as manage big data and overburdened workloads.

Amazon is not only a cloud services company but has

been an online marketplace giant for decades. Through the years it has had to handle and manage its own big data scenarios with the sheer volume of user traffic flowing through their site.

As one might expect, AWS has cloud computing services designed to help an organization efficiently and effectively manage, secure, and run big data applications.

CHAPTER 3
AWS SERVICES

AWS offers a lot of different services that can get quite confusing when it comes to deciding what the best fit for an organization would be. The best way to determine what is going to suit an organization is to look at the most popular services and what they have to offer.

Popular AWS Services

This is a list of the most popular and useful AWS services.

EC2

EC2 is the Elastic Compute Cloud service that gives its users the freedom of low-cost quality services that enable the development as well as the deployment of applications. This service handles these processes quickly and efficiently, giving its users the edge over their competition.

EC2 is also a popular service for the launching of

virtual servers, due to easy scalability and setup.

Elastic computing, for those who are not familiar with the term, is the process of being able to scale computing capabilities on the fly without all the red tape of a conventional system. It gets its name from having the ability to expand and decrease a system's capacity on demand.

VPC

VPC is Amazon's Virtual Private Cloud that works like a Virtual Private Network in the cloud. It is used to ensure the integrity and security of customers' data stored on AWS cloud services.

Amazon VPC makes sure data is secure, as only authorized users will have access to it. This makes AWS a secure environment for their customers.

S3

AWS S3 is short for Amazon Simple Storage Service. This service is one of its main services that offers its customers a simple yet highly efficient and useful storage system. It allows for the storage, retrieval, and sharing of files up to the size of 5TB. Anyone who has tried to store large files on the internet knows how generous that is.

All users or organizations have strict control over their data, who has access to it, and who can use it.

RDS

RDS, or Amazon Relational Database Service, is very popular with developers and it is an SQL database cloud service. RDS offers users many powerful features including being able to access their files at any time from anywhere in the world.

Route 53

The Route 53 service provides an important DNS service to AWS. It was designed to successfully route users to their applications. Route 53 is a service that will convert a website URL to an IP address.

ELB

AWS ELB stands for Elastic Load Balancing, which is very handy to help customers scale the traffic across their cloud-based services. It also offers three different types of load balancers as a service. These load balancers are Application Load Balancer, Classic Load Balancer, and Network Load Balancer.

Auto Scaling

Auto Scaling allows the customer to optimize the way in which they build scaling for automating how different groups across an organization respond to on-demand change. Everything done is automated in AWS Auto Scaling and will automatically set the scale according to the user's preference.

Internet of Things (IoT)

The internet of things is a term used to define all the things that are connected over the internet in certain ways which makes them responsive. Responsive means they connect through various methods like devices, software, coding, etc. to collect and send data.

AWS IoT enables its customers to create various products that can be used across a host of different products. AWS IoT has the ability to connect with its AI services to create smart applications.

AWS 3D, Augmented Reality, and Virtual Reality

Sumerian is Amazon's software that helps customers build and create exciting applications that use 3D, virtual reality, or augmented reality applications.

Now customers can easily create 3D immersible front ends for their applications that will greatly increase brand awareness. Sumerian can also interface with AWS machine learning to connect with applications such as chatbots.

Applications can also be run as a virtual reality or augmented reality for systems and devices that support this function. Virtual reality and 3D can complement each other when leveraging 360° video to create an incredibly real feeling to an application. This is particularly useful for gaming, virtual showings of houses for realtors, and so on.

Augmented reality is fast becoming a trend for companies like furniture stores. Potential customers can choose an item from the store and use augmented reality to see what it could look like in a space in their actual living room.

With AWS, 3D, VR, and AR can be both simple to use and useful for developers to bring another dimension to their applications. VR, 3D, and even AR can also be used in machine learning instances.

CloudFront

The CloudFront service lets the end user know how fast their website is. CloudFront is instrumental in speeding up static and dynamic website content. It will also make static web content a bit faster, which means that any .html, .css, and other image file transfer to users is a lot faster. CloudFront is a secure way to deliver data, videos, applications, and images. The CloudFront service offers high-speed transfers with low latency.

Amazon SQS

SQS or Simple Queue Service is designed to manage message queuing services. Simple Queue Service is capable of sending messages across platforms and multiple services. These services that can have messages sent to them include EC2 instances, S3, and DynamoDB. It makes moving messages from application to application possible, no matter the state of the service (whether it is active or inactive). The SQS service has a visibility timeout of up to 12 hours. The service delivers information by making use of the Java message queue service.

DynamoDB

DynamoDB is a database service on the AWS cloud that is is a NoSQL database that is fully managed. The database supports all Amazon key values and document data structure. It is easy to use and can be used to create various database tables that enable the user to store data in any format as well as quick retrieval thereof. DynamoDB can be used to control the data traffic that spans over multiple servers. It will also monitor the performance tables as well as maintain them.

Redshift

Structured data can be accessed from any existing ODBC, SQL, and JDBC with this fully managed cloud data warehouse service.

Amazon Kinesis

Amazon Kinesis services help end users handle big data running in real-time. Kinesis is able to accept, process, store, and distribute large amounts of data across multiple platforms and consumers. It is able to capture, store, and process data from large sites like social media sites, transactional sites, and subscription sites.

Amazon Glacier

Amazon Glacier plays an important role in an AWS cloud environment. It functions as a web storage service and is a low-cost solution with excellent security features. It can be used for data backup and archival purposes, allowing data to be stored for decades.

Amazon SNS

AWS SNS is a Simple Notification Service that can deliver notifications across platforms to various customers and end users. SNS is designed to distinguish between two types of customers, namely publishers and subscribers, whereby it sends messages to subscribers from various publishers over one of the many supported AWS protocols.

Amazon Elastic Beanstalk

Elastic Beanstalk is popular with developers as they find the service easy to use and quick to deploy applications and services. They can use .NET, Java, PHP, and a number of other programming languages that Elastic Beanstalk supports.

CHAPTER 4
GETTING STARTED WITH
AWS

A
WS has a huge menu of offered services that are divided up into different sections for the convenience of its customers. These can be found from the "Products" section which can be accessed from the main page of the website.

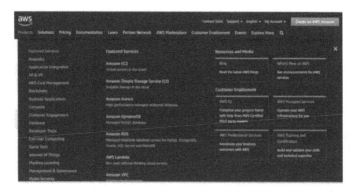

AWS has a massive infrastructure that spans the globe. You can see where their data centers are located by going to the "Global Infrastructure" page.

The orange dots on the page represent new upcoming regions, while the blue dots are current regions. This map is very useful in finding the best region and zone for your business. If you click on the blue dots, they will tell you the region and how many available zones there are in the region.

Where To Start?

Don't let the impressive array of services offered by AWS confuse you. AWS may look or seem extremely complicated, but the fact of the matter is, AWS also has really great tutorials and help facilities. If you get stuck anywhere on the site, simply look for the help button. If you are really stuck, get in contact with their friendly and efficient help desk; they will be more than willing to help you navigate through the startup process if need be.

Planning

The first step in the AWS journey is to scope out exactly what the cloud-based system requirements are.

To do this, spec out the system as if you are going to be installing an on-site networking system. Get all the details of what is required from the system, including the software and services that the system will need to support and run.

Once you have the basics of what the needs are, the scope of the system, and what it is being used for, you then need to figure out the best deployment methods, the best service platform (IaaS, SaaS, PaaS), and hosted services offered by AWS that may be required.

AWS offers a great support service and design team that can help with selecting the best solutions for the organization's needs.

The AWS Screen

The AWS screen is quite a straightforward one. You can browse around at the services and various menu options listed on the site without having to register or login to the site.

Choosing the Correct Package or Service

AWS has an option to help with choosing the correct packages or services. This can be done by browsing through the products. These are broken down into groups pertaining to function. For instance, Analytics has a list of all the analytical services offered by AWS. Each of these services has a more in-depth overview to help the customer better understand their use.

They also have a Featured Services menu selection item which lists their most popular services. Another way to explore the services is to do so by going through the solutions section of the AWS website. The offered services are organized by means of what the hosted system is being used for, by industry, or by organization type.

Once you have a feel for the products and services offered, you will be able to better formulate the requirements for your organization. The next step would be to check out the pricing which lists the various costs and has a convenient section explaining how AWS pricing structure and options work.

Having all the information gathered, the next step is to create an account on AWS, enter all the necessary details, and choose the region, zone, pricing structure, deployment model, and services.

Once the services have been activated, you will receive notification and will be able to get started on the new cloud-based system.

What Are the Zones and Regions?

Amazon has very high-tech data centers that are located in different geographical areas. These geographical areas are the regions, and regions have a few separate locations called availability zones. Local zones are the areas where resources can be placed to make them closer to the end user.

How To Choose a Zone and Region

Availability Zones allow an organization to distribute resources across them so there is no one point of failure in case one of the AWS zones goes down. If a company has instances that have been distributed across multiple zones, failover processes can be built in to make sure outages in one zone can be handled by another zone.

Local Zones allow for the distribution of services to be placed in a zone that is closer to the end user for their convenience. However, local zones are not available in every region. To check if there is a local zone in the required area you need to check on the website under "Geographic Locations."

Regions are where an instance of EC2 servers are hosted. Each region will be in a separate location to each other to ensure system resilience. With isolated instances of services located in various remote regions, AWS can offer a high level of service continuity.

Although regions can be specific to where the

organization is located, regions can be selected for services to be closer to the end user or customer. This means if the client is located in South America, they can have instances located in North America, Europe, and so on.

Always check the pricing and service plan, as there are charges for the transferring of data between the regions.

Creating the Account

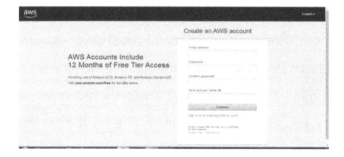

Create an account by selecting the "Sign Up" button on the top right-hand corner of the AWS web page. Enter the email address to be used for account transactions and correspondences. Set up a password and choose the AWS account name, click continue, and follow the instructions that will take you through the setup step by step.

At any time, if you are in need of assistance, AWS help

and support services are available 24/7.

AWS Management Console

AWS has a management console to help users manage and navigate through their services. It is a customizable graphical user interface (GUI) that allows the end user control over selected services. It helps the end user run services such as applications, storage, cloud infrastructure, and any other service they run over the AWS cloud.

EC2 Server

AWS offers many services that are quick and easy to launch at cost-effective prices. Nearly all of AWS packages are scalable and work on an elastic compute basis to ensure they are operating on only the resource amount they need.

The EC2 server is one of the AWS resources that allows customers the convenience of elastic capacity to run applications in the cloud with little overhead and commitment.

EC2: A Quick Overview

EC2 is the AWS elastic compute cloud that gives end users a secure, highly-scalable cloud environment. It gives the customers complete control over their chosen resources and the security of operating within the AWS cloud.

EC2 allows for the establishment of virtual machines for different operating systems to run within the cloud. This increases a company's IT resource capacity, especially for big data and developers. Systems can be tested across multiple platforms without having to invest in expensive equipment to run virtual machines on.

EC2 helps its customers overcome previous compute power limitations they may have had. The fact that the AWS EC2 environment is scalable and elastic means that if a project requires more resources than at first was allocated, it is quick and easy to get more. There is no need for the red tape of change requests or procurement requests; all it takes is re-scaling the resource to meet the current demand. If that demand is no longer required, it is simple enough to scale back down and not pay for resources that are no longer necessary.

The EC2 server is easy to set up, and the process offers a step-by-step solution for the end user to create various instances. Each instance would be an operating platform or service to be run on the EC2 server for the organization. On the EC2 dashboard, the instance can be created by choosing "Create an Instance." Only one instance can be created at a time. Once the instance has been created to work on it, you simply "launch" the instance.

It may take a few minutes for the instance to become active when first created, but once it is, you can switch to it and start using it right away.

Users have a limit of twenty instances per EC2 region. This is the default amount that is set for any account that is created. It is possible to have more than twenty instances running on one EC2 server within a region as long as Amazon has approved it and made allowances for it.

AWS Free Tier & Pricing

The AWS pricing screen has a lot of helpful information on it. All the cloud hosting costs are completely transparent and kept updated. Before you select services, it is advisable to go to the AWS pricing screen. There is a section there that explains the different costs and pricing for various solutions. It also has a section to help an organization optimize its costs as well as a calculator to help calculate various costs.

Free Tier

When first signing up with AWS, unless specified otherwise, the account is set to the free tier option. The free tier has a lot of the available resources and services, but it also has set limits that if exceeded will be billed for.

The free tier expires after a year, but if an organization requires more services than what the limits are for the free tier, these services will be charged to the customer. There are various one-time limits set on some of the services, and all other services that are exceeded get a pay-per-use rate charged. These pay-per-use charges will be the charges as explained in the AWS pricing information.

Small businesses, large enterprises, students, and organizations may all qualify to use the free tier. However, only one user account will be allowed to use the free tier account per organization. It should be noted that any services on the free tier that are used above the free tier limits are charged as a standard fee to the organization. This cost will be added to the total bill, which will include all the AWS accounts associated with an organization.

AWS offers three variations of its free tier. The first is an "always free" tier which has no expiration. The second variation is a short-term trial where end users can test out different services and solutions. And the third variation is the default 12-month free trial which an end user gets upon signing up with AWS.

Pricing

Each service or solution may have its own cost per usage, but AWS does have three standard pricing models.

Pay-as-you-go is the model that allows more flexibility in that you only pay for the service or resources that you need when you need them. For instance, a large project may require extra storage space for the duration of the project. This will be charged while the extra space is being used. When the project is finished and space is no longer required, the charge will be dropped as soon as space is no longer used.

Use more and pay less is a model that can help an organization cut costs for various services with a tiered pricing scheme that provides lower unit costs when you use more. This works similarly to contract pricing structures where buying a contract for two years instead of one saves you a few dollars a month. By opting for a larger storage capacity with S3, you get a tiered pricing scheme where the bigger the storage capacity costs less per unit than a small capacity, though the total cost will be higher.

Reserved instances can cut costs to up to 75% savings. A reserved instance is when an organization invests in an upfront capacity instead of opting for the pay-as-you-go service. This would be similar to leasing equipment of a certain specification where all the configuration is of a certain capacity. This pricing scheme can be cost-saving, as the larger the upfront outlay, the larger the AWS discount is.

CHAPTER 5
AWS MACHINE LEARNING

M achine learning is fast becoming a trend with large corporations as they tend to rely heavily on the organization's data. How the data is processed, organized, and used is of great importance to a company. It can be the key to either falling behind or gaining the marketplace edge over competitors.

What Is Machine Learning?

Machine learning is an application of artificial intelligence whereby a machine learns and can make decisions or recommendations based on the data it is fed. A user will feed information into a computer that it will then sort, process, analyze, and communicate a decision or recommendation based on that data.

There are different methods of machine learning and they are organized under concepts of supervised and unsupervised. The main goal of machine learning is to allow the system to learn and grow on its own without any human assistance or interference.

Artificial Intelligence (AI)

Amazon is no stranger to the AI industry, as they introduced one of the first artificially intelligent, voice-powered virtual assistants, called Alexa. Customers have the opportunity to build an AI application that can enhance their own customer and end user experiences.

One of the great things about AWS AI is that, for many applications, it can be quite easy to use. Thus end users can add various effects such as video analysis, recommendations, forecasting, and virtual assistants without being a specialist in the field. There are different types of AI solutions offered by AWS; most of them are designed around various business functions.

Machine Learning

AWS offers developers SageMaker, which provides a platform for developers to create machine learning (ML) models. To build, train, and deploy a machine learning model in a conventional environment means having to patch together various components and tools. This method is both frustrating, time-consuming, and is at risk of being riddled with errors.

SageMaker is a service that already includes all the tools and components a data scientist or developer would need to build an ML model. AWS ML services are also a lot more cost-effective and not likely to deplete your budget in one swoop.

With the SageMaker suite, developers can label, build, train, tune, deploy, and manage machine learning models in a fraction of the time it would take in a conventional environment.

CHAPTER 6
AWS CERTIFICATIONS

There are eleven AWS certification courses that are broken into four different certification levels from foundation to specialty levels.

Foundation Level Certification

There is only one AWS certification at the foundation level.

AWS Certified Cloud Practitioner

This is an entry-level certification that is designed to give the learner an overall understanding of AWS cloud solutions.

Upon successful completion of the exam, the

certification validates the professional's knowledge of AWS architecture, services, security, support, and understanding of the various pricing options.

AWS Certified Cloud Practitioner course topics include:

- AWS cloud basics

- AWS global infrastructure

- AWS cloud architecture principles

- Key AWS services

- Key AWS services use cases

- Understand the basics of deploying an AWS environment

- Understanding of the basics of operating in an AWS environment

- Understanding of the basics of AWS security

- Understanding the various compliance aspects of AWS

- A clear understanding of the different pricing models, structure, and billing procedures

Recommended entry requirements for the certification:

- A basic understanding of networking

- At least six months to a year's experience in an IT environment

- Basic understanding of cloud-based systems

Exam Information:

- Only available at authorized AWS test centers

- Multiple-choice questions

- Duration is 1 hour and 30 minutes

Associate Level Certification

There are 3 AWS certifications at the associate level.

AWS Certified Solutions Architect

This certification is the next level up from the foundation level and takes a more in-depth look at the AWS cloud. In this course, the student will be introduced to the key AWS services, such as VPC, S3, EC2, IAM, and Route 53. It is the student's introduction to the power in these services and teaches the various AWS approaches to security, networking, and storage, as well as compute possibilities.

AWS Certified Solutions Architect course topics include:

- How to design a robust AWS infrastructure based on AWS solutions

- How to deploy a successful AWS networking solution

- Learning the basic principles of AWS solution architecture

Recommended entry requirements for the certification:

- Entry-level experience in data storage solutions

- Experience in database operations

- Understanding of compute services

- Understanding of networking services

- Some experience in systems infrastructure design

- Some experience in the management and deployment of systems

- AWS foundation certification

Exam Information:

- Only available at authorized AWS test centers

- Multiple-choice questions

- Duration is 2 hours and 10 minutes

AWS Certified Developer

This certification is not only for developers; it is for anyone who wants a more in-depth knowledge of AWS services. This course covers AWS services that are development-specific, such as Elastic Beanstalk, SQS, SNS, and DynamoDB. Basic knowledge of SDKs and APIs will be advantageous for this certification.

AWS Certified Developer course topics include:

- AWS SDKs and APIs

- AWS architecture

- Application development in an AWS cloud environment

- Application deployment in an AWS cloud environment

Recommended entry requirements for the certification:

- High-level programming language knowledge

- Basic knowledge of SDKs and APIs

- Basic knowledge of command-line interfaces (CLIs)

- Basic knowledge of software development lifecycles

- Basic knowledge of how to use the key AWS services

- AWS foundation certification

Exam Information:

- Only available at authorized AWS test centers

- Multiple-choice questions

- Duration is 1 hour and 20 minutes

AWS Certified SysOps Administrator

This course covers AWS services such as CloudWatch

and teaches the student the fundamentals of AWS architecture and how to put them into practice. The SysOps Admin Certification course is the highest certification level in the associate certification level. It is quite a lot harder than the other associate certifications. As far as AWS associate certifications go, the SysOps Administrator is one that is highly sought after in the job market. The certification can be taken by anyone interested in becoming a SysOps administrator and who has some hands-on experience in the IT infrastructure field.

AWS Certified SysOps Administrator course topics include:

- How to deploy services and applications in an AWS environment

- How to operate services and applications in an AWS environment

- How to manage services and applications in an AWS environment

- How to design and implement a robust AWS infrastructure

- How to successfully scope the deployment method for an organization

- How to successfully scope the services an organization would need based on their case study

Recommended entry requirements for the certification:

- Basic understanding of AWS tenets for cloud architecture

- Foundation certification for AWS

- Be able to manage, design, deploy and maintain an IT systems infrastructure

- Basic understanding of virtualization platforms

Exam Information:

- Only available at authorized AWS test centers

- Multiple-choice questions

- Duration is 1 hour and 20 minutes

Professional Level Certification

There are two professional level certifications for AWS.

AWS Certified Solutions Architect

This is a more advanced Certified Solutions Architect course and exam. It requires a more in-depth knowledge of both IT systems and AWS cloud solutions. It also requires the student to have at least two years of hands-on experience using AWS.

AWS Certified System Architect course topics include:

- How to leverage the AWS platform in order to build robust, reliable, and secure applications

- Networking technologies vs. AWS' networking platform

- Learning how to deploy and implement hybrid cloud methods

Recommended entry requirements for the certification:

- At least two years of hands-on experience working in an AWS cloud environment

- Experience with AWS cloud architecture

- Versed in AWS scripting language

- Be able to successfully design, and implement applications

- Must be able to confidently assess an application to pinpoint any architectural restructuring needs

- At least one associate level certification.

- AWS foundation certification

Exam Information:

- Only available at authorized AWS test centers

- Multiple-choice questions

- Duration is 2 hours and 50 minutes

AWS Certified DevOps Engineer

This certification course leverages the concepts of DevOps to streamline the automation process of managing and deploying software applications.

AWS Certified DevOps Engineer course topics include:

- Implementing a successful continuous delivery system in an AWS environment

- Implement a successful management system in an

AWS environment

- Manage and maintain the automation tools of the operational process in an AWS environment

- Implement scalable solutions utilizing the available AWS services

Recommended entry requirements for the certification:

- Hands-on experience in storage, database, compute, and networking services

- Ability to identify which service meets the user requirements

- Knowledge of how to manage and deploy service

- AWS foundation certification

- At least one AWS association certification

Exam Information:

- Only available at authorized AWS test centers

- Multiple-choice questions

- Duration is 2 hours and 50 minutes

Specialty Level Certification

There are five specialty-level certifications for AWS.

AWS Certified Security

This specialty certification covers the fundamentals of security in an AWS environment. It covers topics from incident logging and response to data protection, infrastructure security, encryption, systems monitoring, management, and reporting.

AWS Certified Security course topics include:

- Learning the AWS tools and services for security

- Protecting sensitive data in an AWS environment and the tools needed to do so

- Data protection best practices and encryption mechanisms

- How to implement monitoring and logging systems to pinpoint security vulnerabilities

Recommended entry requirements for the certification:

- At least two years of hands-on experience in storage, database, compute, and networking services

- Knowledge of data, internet, and infrastructure security

- AWS foundation certification

- At least one AWS association certification

- At least one AWS professional certification

Exam Information:

- Only available at authorized AWS test centers

- Multiple-choice questions

- Duration is 2 hours and 50 minutes

AWS Certified Big Data

The AWS Certified Big Data is a specialty certification that requires development or data analytics or data scientific skill level. This certificate demonstrates the student's ability to understand big data and the architecture thereof.

AWS Certified Big Data course topics include:

- AWS big data services for architecting in order to implement best practices

- Designing big data

- Maintaining big data

- Introduction to AWS tools for automating data analysis

- Using the AWS tool to automate data analysis

- Best practices for big data security

- Overview of AWS services such as Athena, Rekognition, and Quicksight

Recommended entry requirements for the certification:

- A background in data analytics

- Experience designing the architecture for big data specifically in an AWS environment using AWS big data services

- AWS foundation certification

- At least one AWS association certification

- At least one AWS professional certification

Exam Information:

- Only available at authorized AWS test centers

- Multiple-choice questions

- Duration is 2 hours and 50 minutes

AWS Certified Advanced Networking

This specialty certification validates the professional's experience and skill set for performing complex networking tasks in an AWS environment. It specifically pays attention to the hybrid IT networking architecture at scale. Candidates should have a background in architecting and implementing network solutions and advanced knowledge of networking on AWS.

AWS Certified Advanced Networking course topics include:

- Designing AWS infrastructure cloud solutions

- Developing an AWS infrastructure cloud solution

- Deploying AWS cloud solutions within an AWS environment

- Developing architectural best practices for the implementation of core services in an AWS environment

- AWS tasks for automation of network

deployments

- Security and compliance in an AWS environment.

- How to optimize the network and best troubleshooting practices

Recommended entry requirements for the certification:

- Knowledge of complex networking infrastructure

- Knowledge of complex networking tasks in an AWS environment

- Knowledge of hybrid IT networking architecture

- Must understand how to scale hybrid IT networking architecture

- A background in architecting network solutions is advantageous

- Knowledge of implementing network solutions in an AWS environment

- AWS foundation certification

- At least one AWS association certification

- At least one AWS professional certification

Exam Information:

- Only available at authorized AWS test centers

- Multiple-choice questions

- Duration is 2 hours and 50 minutes

AWS Certified Machine Learning

This specialty certification course covers how to maintain, implement, and create machine learning solutions across platforms in an AWS environment.

AWS Certified Cloud Practitioner course topics include:

- Choosing the best approach for ML in a given organizational case study

- How to identify the best AWS solutions in order to create an ML solution in an AWS environment

- How to identify the best AWS solutions to deploy an ML solution in an AWS environment

- Designing and developing a reliable, secure, and scalable ML solution in an AWS environment

Recommended entry requirements for the certification:

- At least two years working in an AWS environment

- A background in a development or data science role

- One to two years of experience in an ML or deep learning environment

- Knowledge of ML or Deep learning in an AWS environment

- AWS foundation certification

- At least one AWS association certification

- At least one AWS professional certification

Exam Information:

- Only available at authorized AWS test centers

- Multiple-choice questions

- Duration is 2 hours and 50 minutes

AWS Certified Alexa Skill Builder

This specialty certification demonstrates a professional technical ability to create, test, and deploy development designs using Alexa Skill builder.

AWS Certified Cloud Practitioner course topics include:

- The core value of voice

- The user design experience

- Best practices for Alexa security

- Hands-on lab environment to work on the Alexa Developer Console

Recommended entry requirements for the certification:

- At least two years of experience working in an AWS environment

- At least two years of experience working in AI

- Knowledge of Alexa or AI in an AWS environment

- AWS foundation certification

- At least one AWS association certification

- At least one AWS professional certification

Exam Information:

- Only available at authorized AWS test centers

- Multiple-choice questions

- Duration is 2 hours and 50 minutes

CHAPTER 7
AWS VERSUS THE REST

AWS is an industry leader in the cloud hosting race and comes out tops for its innovative services, solutions, flexible payment structures, and global reach.

This chapter takes a look at how AWS compares to some of the other large cloud hosting solutions on the market today.

Microsoft Azure

Microsoft versus Amazon cloud services can be a difficult decision, as they are both popular cloud-based solutions.

When it comes to configuring EC2 versus the pre-configured VMS of Azure, AWS EC2 gives the most flexibility because it can be configured on the fly. Azure's VMS requires end users to choose a virtual hard disk. The VMS is then pre-configured by the third party. This means that the end user has to give specific memory and cores that are required for their Azure VMS environment.

AWS offers a more flexible and elastic temporary storage solution, and this storage is only assigned when the instance that is started calls for it. When the instance no longer needs the storage, it is destroyed. For Azure users, Microsoft offers temporary storage but as by block storage. For object storage in Azure, this is done through Block Blobs and for VMS storage it is done through page Blobs.

AWS Virtual Private Cloud operates by allowing the end user to create isolated networks within the AWS cloud environment. Azure has a virtual network that creates isolated subnets, allocates private IP address ranges, and networks. This is pretty much the same as AWS VPC.

Azure is more accommodating when it comes to hybrid cloud systems. Azure tends to shy away from third-party cloud providers.

In their pricing models, AWS and Azure both follow a pay-as-you-go pricing structure. But AWS charges per hour while Azure tends to charge per minute, making it a more exacting pricing structure.

AWS has many more features, services, and flexible

configuration solutions. It can easily be customized and can offer a lot with various tools offered by third parties. On the other hand, Azure is quite easy to use for pretty much anyone who knows how to use Windows. Customers can make a hybrid cloud to an on-premise Windows server environment.

Both AWS and Azure have a lot to offer their customers, but which one to choose will be what best suits the company's needs. AWS provides Infrastructure as a Service (IaaS) plus a wide range of products and services. But if you are looking for Platform as a Service (Paas), Azure has a lot of added benefits.

Rackspace

Rackspace and AWS have been around for the same amount of time, and Rackspace is a very popular cloud hosting environment. AWS EC2 and Rackspace offer the same service with pretty much the same tools. The one difference is in the pricing structures, as Rackspace has been known to be a bit more expensive than AWS.

As far as infrastructure services AWS EC2 and Rackspace are very similar. Both platforms offer a host of affordable services and solutions. AWS has more to offer developers in terms of resources with their Cloud9 IDE and ECS container platform service.

There are some managed services that are offered by Rackspace that are not offered by AWS. And you can, in fact, obtain managed services through Rackspace to support AWS infrastructure.

As a multi-cloud environment, you could easily use Rackspace managed services while taking advantage of all the benefits of using AWS EC2 instances. As these companies are adding new features, running a multi-cloud environment is becoming more and more popular. This is due to the fact that you get to have the best of all cloud-based hosting.

With a little extra management power and all the right tools, it is not that hard to run multi-cloud architectures.

Google Cloud

The choice between AWS and Google Cloud is a tough one, as they both have their good points as well as their downfalls.

For larger enterprises with established needs, AWS would be the better choice of the two environments. AWS has a global presence, so it is a perfect choice for multinational companies looking for a service that spans beyond the United States and Europe. AWS also has state-of-the-art security features, has more resilience, and offers a high level of support.

But Google Cloud has sweetened the pot with its very generous free tier offer. It also has even greater flexibility than AWS and has one of the best prices for cloud hosting solutions. Google Cloud also has an excellent variety of services to offer its clients.

If you want to take advantage of the services of Google Cloud and/or Azure along with AWS, this can be done in a multi-cloud environment. Running a multi-cloud environment allows you to pick and choose each service from the cloud host that fits your needs.

DigitalOcean

There is not much competition when comparing DigitalOcean to AWS. This is because DigitalOcean targets a different customer base. DigitalOcean targets smaller developers in need of an instance or instances that are small but able to accommodate high-performance systems.

AWS is a much larger company and runs its cloud hosting services on a broader scale, targeting the larger marketplace and mixed environments.

DigitalOcean does tend to outperform AWS in VM performance, giving their users an easy-to-use interface that is basically a clean slate to start working on. They also have limited services that do not overwhelm their users with the giant list AWS offers. And they offer developers the convenience of one-click deployments.

With AWS IaaS and PaaS, there is a whole menu of mind-boggling services to pick and choose from. It can be as exciting as it can be confusing to the end user. Unless you are a developer looking for a clean, fast solution, AWS has more to offer. But as a whole, they are not really companies that you could compare since they each offer the customer differing solutions for specific needs.

IBM Cloud

IBM has been in the IT business a lot longer than Amazon. They have gone from large mainframe and AS400s to modern-day technology. It only stands to reason that when it comes to business solutions they will give AWS a run for their money with cloud hosting.

IBM also has the brand name that gives them a competitive edge, as their names has become basically synonymous with computing. IBM does have some advantages over AWS in cloud hosting, with its flexible configurations, monitoring system, and management solutions.

Still, AWS has the advantage with the sheer volume of services and solutions it has to offer at very reasonable prices.

Oracle Cloud

When it comes to pricing, Oracle cloud has the edge on AWS, with their price-to-performance available for some of their services. Other than that, they are pretty much similar in that Oracle cloud is also well-suited to the needs of large enterprises. Both IBM and AWS offer high-level security, stability, reliability, scalability, and hybrid applications. For Oracle applications, the Oracle cloud may be the better solution, as both Oracle and AWS offer a host of suitable solutions for developers.

VMware

One cannot really compare VMware Cloud or AWS, at least not since they formed an alliance where AWS hosted the VMWare Cloud. This adds a whole new dimension to both AWS and VMware. AWS customers now have an on-demand service offering vSphere cloud-based solutions. VMware benefits from being able to offer its customers not only applications within the vSphere cloud but also access to the wide range of AWS services.

The service is operated by the VMware Cloud Foundation. It offers all the familiar VMware tools such as VMware vSAN, WMware vCenter management, VMware vSphere, and VMware NSX. IT teams that are familiar with VMware will have no problems managing the VMware cloud-based system. All the IT team's familiar VMware tools have been optimized to run on AWS elastic infrastructure. This infrastructure is offered on a private cloud, giving the customer all the power of a dedicated AWS bare-metal environment.

Together AWS and VMware have created a powerful tool that leverages both private and public cloud environments which are beneficial to both organizations.

CloudWays

CloudWays is a cloud hosting company that is popular amongst those looking for a fast, reliable, and easy solution to cloud hosting websites. Instead of having to go through all the technical jargon while trying to set up a cloud-based platform, CloudWays gives a simple point and click solution. It helps a person with limited technical abilities navigate a technical framework like a pro.

It also offers its customers the choice to host their web-services on all the major cloud-based hosting companies, including AWS. CloudWays is the bridge between those customers that need cloud computing but are not very technical.

Alibaba Cloud

Not a lot of people outside of China have heard about Alibaba Cloud, which was the country's main cloud-based marketplace up until 2015. But Alibaba Cloud is fast becoming a force to be reckoned with in the cloud hosting arena. They have also been around since 2009, which is only a few years after AWS.

Alibaba Cloud mainly focused on China and its neighboring countries until a large cash infusion into the company allowed it to expand to the United States. It opened its doors in the US in 2015 and soon after that stretched its global reach into Europe during 2016.

Alibaba offers much the same services as AWS and their pricing structures vary depending on the required service or services that are needed. While Alibaba can offer most of the services to its customers that AWS can, it is not as widely recognized as a brand name. Alibaba does not currently have the geographical presence that AWS has, although Alibaba has big plans to increase its geographical reach in the near future. Alibaba may soon be running neck and neck with the global giant AWS.

CHAPTER 8
INTERESTING FACTS ABOUT AMAZON AND AWS

There are not many people using the internet who do not know who or what Amazon is. Yet, as prevalent in most people's lives as the company is, not many people know a lot of the story behind the online retail giant.

A Few Facts About Amazon

A Humble Online Bookstore

Amazon started as a small online bookstore back in 1995 when Jeff Bezos began to sell books from his garage. The oversized mailbox he installed to handle all the mail for his new start-up can still be seen at the address where he first started his online business.

Fluid Concepts and Creative Analogies

The first book Amazon ever sold was by author Doug Hofstadter on April 3, 1995.

The Ringing of the Bell

When Amazon was still a young company, they would ring a bell every time a sale was made. Of course, eventually the company's sales expanded to such an extent that the bell was rung far too often, so the ritual was stopped.

The First Month

Amazon sold a book to people in 45 different countries and at least one in every North American state within their first month of business.

Relentless.com

Jeff Bezos had no actual plans to name his site Amazon. His first choice was vetoed by his lawyer, and his second choice was Relentless. If you go to Relentless.com, you will get automatically forwarded to Amazon's website.

Fiona

Fiona was what the Amazon Kindle was originally going to be called. Fiona was to be named after a character in a book called *The Diamond Age*, a sci-fi novel written by Neal Stephenson.

Kiva Systems

Amazon took over Kiva Systems in 2012. Kiva Systems developed smart machines that are capable of retrieving and delivering various items. There are around 45,000 of these machines working Amazon warehouses.

Most Valuable Retailer

Amazon is said to be a lot more valuable than some of the big retail stores like Wal-Mart, JCPenny, Sears, and Target. Not only is it more valuable than all of them on their own but also with them all combined. Amazon is worth around $350 billion.

Amazon Owns Whole Foods

In 2017 Amazon purchased the organic and natural food products chain, Whole Food.

Audible, Twitch, and Goodreads

Amazon owns Audible, which is a book cataloging site. It also owns Twitch, which is a live streaming site, and GoodReads, the book review website.

The Bottom Line

Although Amazon took off with quite a boom, it did not actually show any net profit until 2004.

40-Minute Downtime Glitch

Amazon's website went down for a total of 40 minutes in August of 2013. The downtime costs Amazon $120,000 per minute, with an overall estimated loss of $4.8 million.

722 New AWS Services in One Year

AWS is forever adding new services to its ever-increasing list of services they have to offer their customers. In one year, AWS added 722 new services and features to its platform.

AWS Has a Large Education Customer Base

AWS has millions of customers worldwide with 5,000 of those customers being educational institutions.

GoDaddy Uses AWS

GoDaddy, one of the world's largest website hosting companies in the world, recently moved its services over to AWS.

Aurora Is Trending

Aurora is one of AWS's fastest-growing database services and has fast been catching up to Oracle, which has dominated the database world for decades.

What Is AWS?

AWS is one of the largest cloud hosting services in the world, with a presence in over 190 countries. Most people will visit a site that is hosted by AWS at least once a day. But still, ⅔ of Americans have no idea what AWS is.

Large Customer Base

AWS has over 1 million customers worldwide and is growing rapidly by the day. It also holds the most market share for cloud hosting facilities, with Microsoft coming in second and IBM trailing behind Microsoft.

Government Agencies Have Adopted AWS WorldWide

AWS has a client base of over 600 government agencies across the globe.

Cloud Data Centers by 2021

It is said that by 2021, the majority of workloads will be processed by cloud data centers.

CHAPTER 9

AWS INTERVIEW QUESTIONS

AWS Engineers are currently right at the top of the highest paying IT jobs.

There are eleven different AWS certifications and four different levels of certifications. They are worth the time, effort, and money in order to land a top AWS position. But even with a certificate in-hand and years of experience under your belt, you are still going to answer the AWS interview questions.

Top AWS Interview Questions

Here are some of the top AWS interview questions.

Question: Explain AWS Region.

Answer: An AWS Region is a geographical area that is separate from any other region. Each region will have one or more locations that are isolated from the others, called availability zones. These regions and zones are designed for low-latency high fault tolerance.

Question: Explain IAM components.

Answer: IAM components:

- There is the IAM User that is the person who will be using AWS services and will use the AWS Management Console to maintain, manage, and operate within an AWS environment.

- The IAM Group allows members of the group to be assigned rights to specific tasks, applications, features, services, and functions. Instead of assigning rights at an individual level, they can be assigned once at a group level. This makes it easier to manage and maintain users' rights and privileges

- The IAM Role is a role that is an identity to which is granted certain permissions to perform certain tasks. It is not a user but rather a specific role. For instance, a manager of Payroll can access Payroll at a higher level than a member in the Payroll group. If the manager was then assigned another position, their user ID would simply be removed from the role.

- IAM Permission are assigned according to identity-based or resource-based type permissions.

- IAM Policy is where the user permissions list is documented in JSON Format. This policy can be assigned to a group, role, or user.

Question: Can you list the features of Amazon S3?

Answer: Amazon S3 features include:

- unlimited storage for files

- varied size up to 5 terabytes

- buckets to store files, with each bucket having a unique identifying name

- object-based storage

Question: What is CloudWatch?

Answer: CloudWatch is an AWS environment monitoring service that monitors AWS cloud resources.

Question: List some of the CloudWatch Options.

Answer: Some of the CloudWatch Options are:

- CloudWatch can store and monitor EC2 instances generated logs.

- The log data can be stored for a period of time that conforms with company policy for the retention of data.

- The CloudWatch Dashboard option allows for the creation of visual statistics in the form of charts and graphs, which is handy for the monitoring of applications and resources.

- CloudWatch has threshold alarms that can be set to monitor the performance of a system and send out an alert when the threshold is either reached or exceeded.

- Another option of CloudWatch is the ability to set up events to be triggered when an alarm goes off, and it can be designed specifically for certain alarms. When the alarm goes off, the system will know to take action as per the alarm specification.

Question: List use cases for Lambda.

Answer: Lambda use cases:

- As a web application, Lambda can easily be integrated with other AWS services. This will give the end user the power to create a scalable web application.

- Lambada can be used to run a specific code that can trigger an event when a certain device or software comes online.

- AWS Lambda can be used to develop backend mobile applications.

- When used in conjunction with Kinesis, it is possible to create an application for the processing of real-time streaming data.

Question: Explain how costing works with an Elastic IP address (EIP).

Answer: One Elastic IP address attached to the active instance does not get charged. But costs will be incurred under the following conditions:

- If there are more than one Elastic IPs per instance

- If an Elastic IP is attached to an inactive

instance

- If an Elastic IP does not have an instance attached to it

Question: Explain the Amazon S3 tiers.

Answer: S3 storage tiers are as follows:

- The standard tier is used for files that are used often and must have instant access.

- The standard tier for infrequent access; this is storage for data that needs to be accessed quickly, but only as and when required. Otherwise, it is stored for the maximum available time that meets compliance standards for the organization.

Question: List the CloudFront events that can cause a trigger.

Answer: CloudFront events can be triggered by:

- Any HTTP/HTTPS access request on CloudFront can trigger an event at an Edge Location. And edge locations is one that is closer to the end user for more convenience, ease of access, and faster download/upload times.

- A CloudFront ready to receive motion.

Question: What are the two main types of volume provided by Amazon EBS?

Answer: The two main EBS volume types are:

- a solid-state drive (SSD) volume that is more expensive than a hard disk drive. It tends to be more reliable than a hard disk drive and is therefore suited for work in which there are frequent read and write requests.

- The hard disk drive (HDD) volume is the cheaper of the two options. It is more suited to high volume throughput or streaming workload.

Question: Can you explain AWS?

Answer: Amazon Web Services is a collection of web hosting services, applications, and solutions for a seamless cost-effective cloud hosting solution for organizations.

Questions: Can you name some of the key services available from AWS?

Answer: Some of the key AWS services are:

- Elastic Cloud Compute or EC2 is an on-demand cloud computing resource that can host applications across multiple instances.

- Elastic Block Services or EBS, which is a storage solution for EC2 services that allows for the storage of data from an EC2 instance that can be kept after the instance has been destroyed.

- Identity and Access Management services add security to the end user's AWS account.

- Route53 is a DNS web service for the AWS environment.

Question: Do you know how many buckets can be created in AWS by default?

Answer: AWS allows each user account within an organization to create 100 buckets.

Question: Can you explain what key-pair in AWS is?

Answer: It is a form of extra login security which requires both a public key and private key to access the account.

Question: Can you name the different types of instances?

Answer: These are the different types of instances:

- Accelerated computing instance

- Computer-optimized instance

- General-purpose instance

- Memory-optimized instance

- Storage optimized instance

Question: Can you explain what VPC is?

Answer: Virtual Private Cloud is a logically separated network that is in the AWS cloud. It is customizable and has its own security groups, subnets, gateways, etc.

Question: What are the different AWS deployment methods?

Answer: There are four different types of deployment methods:

- Private Cloud

- Public Cloud

- Hybrid Cloud

- Community Cloud

Question: What are the different AWS cloud services?

Answer: There are four types of cloud services offered by AWS:

- Data as a Service (DaaS)

- Infrastructure as a Service (IaaS)

- Platform as a Service (PaaS)

- Software as a Service (SaaS)

Question: Explain Data as a Service.

Answer: Data as a Service is a way of leveraging the extensive storage capacity as well as data security of the cloud. Usually used for critical information that an organization needs to be able to access where and whenever they need, but it is not necessarily data that is accessed all the time. Mostly historical data that needs to be kept for auditing and financial record purposes, legal documentation, and so on.

Data as a Service is a relatively new service to be

offered on a cloud hosting platform.

Question: What are the benefits of Data as a Service?

Answer: There are a few benefits for Data as a Service.

- DaaS offers agility: Data is a company's number one asset, and in today's world there is a massive amount of it. For organizations, this means having to store and archive these massive amounts of data. A lot of data does not need to be accessed every day or even for years, but still it needs to be kept, and it needs to be available for quick access as and when needed. To this purpose, DaaS offers quick access to stored data in the cloud from anywhere.

- DaaS is cost-effective: A company does not have to fork out money to buy extra data storage solutions and backup solutions. Most storage solutions in a cloud environment can also be scaled and have a cost-effective payment structure.

Question: Explain the AWS Cloud Architecture layers.

Answer: The AWS Cloud Architecture layers are:

- The cloud controller

- The cloud cluster controller

- The cloud storage controller

- The cloud node controller

Question: Can you name some of the database engines AWS RDS can use?

Answer: AWS RDS database engineers are:

- OracleDB

- MYSQL

- MS-SQL

- PostgreDB

- MariaDB

Question: What are some of the most popular AWS features?

Answer: Some of the most popular AWS features include:

- Amazon EC2

- Amazon Simple Storage Service (S3)

- Amazon Aurora

- Amazon Sagemaker

- Amazon VPC

- AWS Lambda

- Amazon RDS

- Amazon DynamoDB

Question: Can you explain what Amazon CloudFront Geo Restriction is?

Answer: Geo restriction is a way to restrict geographical access to certain users in certain areas to stop them from accessing data from that area, services, and so on.

Question: Can you explain what SQS is?

Answer: SQS stands for Simple Queuing Services, which is a service that acts as a buffer between two controllers.

Question: Can you explain auto scaling and its advantages?

Answer: Auto scaling is a means by which AWS ensures that systems always have enough capacity in order to function at their optimum, unrestricted capacity. The following are the benefits of auto scaling:

- Auto scaling is cost-effective, as customers can dynamically scale capacity to their current needs.

- Launching EC2 instances can be done on an as-needed basis, and the service will only be charged for instances that are being used.

- When an instance is no longer needed, it is destroyed, and the organization will no longer be billed for it.

- Auto scaling allows for better fault tolerance in that if an instance becomes unstable, auto scaling will detect the fault and instantly destroy the instance. It will also recreate the instance in a healthy environment.

- Auto scaling can also be configured across multiple zones to ensure system resilience. If one zone goes down, it can automatically switch to another zone with almost seamless precision.

Question: Can you explain snowball?

Answer: Snowball is an option for the data transport of large files or massive amounts of data. Snowball is fast and efficient; it is also extremely cost-effective.

Question: Can you explain what a subnet is?

Answer: A subnet is a subdivision on an IP address. A company, for instance, will be allocated a certain amount of IP address ranges, and in order to ensure there are enough addresses to accommodate the entire organization, these addresses are broken down into subnets.

Question: Describe some connections issues that could arise while connecting to an instance.

Answer: Some connecting issue to instances are:

- Connection timed out errors are common errors.

- The server does not recognize a user key.

- Access is denied due to a host key not found.

- A private key file is unprotected.

- "No supported authentication method available"

Question: Why use an AWS Storage Gateway ?

Answer: An AWS Storage Gateway (ASG) has the following uses:

- ASG is a great facility to create stable and secure backup systems.

- Data can easily be backed up from any local storage to the cloud.

- ASG offers on-demand backup and restore options.

- It is a more robust, secure, and reliable backup solution than a tape-based backup system.

- ASG offers variable or elastic storage solutions. This means that storage can expand and contract with a company's immediate needs.

- There is no physical equipment needed, as

everything is done through the cloud and hosted on AWS data center servers.

- ASG has the option to create full system snapshots of local devices to ensure fast restoring time and great system continuity.

- Disaster recovery and fallback times are a lot less than conventional disaster recovery and fallback procedures.

- ASG allows for Hybrid Cloud solutions across platforms such as deployment methods or onsite systems and cloud-based systems.

CONCLUSION

AWS offers a whole host of services that may have not been covered in this book or that have been released after the time this book was published. It is always best to check for the latest updates on the AWS website.

By now you should have a better understanding of cloud computing—what it is, what it is used for, and how it works. You should also have a much broader knowledge of AWS. This knowledge should include how it works and why so many companies are moving towards AWS or at least to cloud-based services in general.

AWS is a powerful tool to help an organization of any size reach great heights through intelligent, fast access and scalable solutions designed to suit nearly every entity's needs and budget.

Although the system can significantly cut costs, it cannot cut down on the planning phase. This is the phase that involves doing the research, deciding on the correct deployment method, and researching ASW services to suit your organization's needs.

Even in the early planning stages, Amazon Web Services Websites can be very helpful, filled with tools to help make every function easy, every step of the way through the cloud-based lifecycle.

AWS has a library of useful resources, documentation, and training materials to make the end user's experience on their cloud hosting service as easy and seamless as possible.

If you have read through all of the chapters in this book, you should have a better understanding of AWS. This book covered what AWS has to offer, how it compares to other similar services, and what you can expect of the pricing packages. For those of you looking into a career as an AWS professional, there is a list of common interview questions to help prepare you for those tough AWS interviews.

As big data, machine learning, and AI are becoming more popular, it is in your best interest to do a deeper dive into the subject. Although this guide has given you a brief introduction into what you can expect of ML and AI on the AWS cloud, machine learning is a highly specialized field that holds much more for developers and data scientists. But there are some regions of AI that are easy to operate and work well with AWS services and applications.

AWS continues to grow each year, and this past year was no exception. Nor is it only the company that is growing either, as more businesses are turning toward cloud hosting facilities and growing because of them. This is due to the Lean Six Sigma, Agile, DevOps, and other organizations looking for ways to cut costs and create a more productive working environment. Cloud-based infrastructure and their software solutions fit right into this methodology, since they are a way to cut down on overhead and create a better way to connect to the office from wherever a person is in the world.

REFERENCES

Amazon Web Services LLC. (2011). File:AWS Simple Icons AWS Cloud.svg - Wikimedia Commons [Photograph]. Retrieved from https://commons.wikimedia.org/wiki/File:AWS_Simple_Icons_AWS_Cloud.svg

ARPANET UNITED STATES DEFENSE PROGRAM. (n.d.). Retrieved from https://www.britannica.com/topic/ARPANET

Bourne, J. (2014, May 06). Step back in time: AT&T predicts the cloud in 1993. Retrieved from https://www.cloudcomputing-news.net/news/2014/may/06/step-back-time-t-predicts-cloud-1993/

Definition — What does Compuserve mean? (n.d.). Retrieved from https://www.techopedia.com/definition/6578/compuserve

Forrest, C. (2015, November 11). 15 high profile companies that run on top of Amazon Web Services.

Retrieved from https://www.techrepublic.com/pictures/photos-15-high-profile-companies-that-run-on-top-of-amazon-web-services/2/

Hall, K. (2019, August 06). Amazon Web Services doubled its footprint in the UK and will only get bigger, reckon analysts. Retrieved from https://www.theregister.co.uk/2019/08/06/aws_doubles_uk_footprint_sits_review/

History of the Web. (n.d.). Retrieved from https://webfoundation.org/about/vision/history-of-the-web/?gclid=EAIaIQobChMIocXWy_Ts5gIVS7TtCh1GdAu8EAAYASAAEgISF_D_BwE

Hofstadter, D. R. (1996). Fluid Concepts And Creative Analogies: Computer Models Of The Fundamental Mechanisms Of Thought (1st ed.). USA: Basic Books.

Howell, E. (2018, July 17). Curiosity Rover: Facts and Information. Retrieved from https://www.space.com/17963-mars-curiosity.html

Internet Hall of Fame Pioneer J.C.R. Licklider. (n.d.). Retrieved from https://internethalloffame.org/inductees/jcr-licklider

Larken, A. (2019, June 6). The 11 AWS Certifications: Which is Right for You and Your Team? Retrieved from https://cloudacademy.com/blog/choosing-the-right-aws-certification/

Lyle. (n.d.). Public Domain Clip Art Image | file server | ID: 13935568227899 | PublicDomainFiles.com [Photograph]. Retrieved from http://www.publicdomainfiles.com/show_file.php?id=13935568227899

Networking: Vision and Packet Switching 1959 - 1968 Intergalactic Vision to Arpanet. (n.d.). Retrieved from http://www.historyofcomputercommunications.info/Book/2/2.1-IntergalacticNetwork_1962-1964.html

OpenClipart. (n.d.-a). Application server vector drawing [Photograph]. Retrieved from https://freesvg.org/application-server-vector-drawing

OpenClipart. (n.d.-b). Connected globe vector icon | Free SVG [Photograph]. Retrieved from https://freesvg.org/connected-globe-vector-icon

OpenClipart. (n.d.-c). Vector drawing of database

134

server | Public domain vectors [Photograph]. Retrieved from https://publicdomainvectors.org/en/free-clipart/Vector-drawing-of-database-server/13558.html

OSDE8Info. (2009). AWS EC2 Management Console [Photograph]. Retrieved from https://www.flickr.com/photos/osde-info/3379281738

Regions, Availability Zones, and the Local Zone. (n.d.). Retrieved from https://docs.aws.amazon.com/AWSEC2/latest/UserGuide/using-regions-availability-zones.html

SilverStartalk - Made using Dia, CC BY 2.5. (2019). Computer network diagram [Photograph]. Retrieved from https://en.wikipedia.org/wiki/Computer_network_diagram#/media/File:Sample-network-diagram.png

srip. (n.d.). Backup Icon - 2345368 [Photograph]. Retrieved from https://www.flaticon.com/free-icon/backup_2345368?term=backup page=1&position=24

What is Big Data? (n.d.). Retrieved from https://aws.amazon.com/big-data/what-is-big-data/